Getting to know

SANTORINI

COMPLETE TOURIST GUIDE - 150 COLOUR PHOTOGRAPHS

© editions D.HAITALIS, 30 CHRISSALIDOS St., ATHENS, TEL: 2523511

Contents

*P*rologue

*It looks like a ship sailing in the middle
of the Aegean Sea.
Proudly raising its prow to the elements that
scarred it. With the passage of time, only half of
it remains.
But this loss has given it its incomparable beauty.*

*Santorini.
The island linked with the legend of the lost Atlantis.
The island with chronicles of Biblical catastrophes
engraved in its memory.*

*Santorini.
The only Aegean island where survival was a dare.
A constant struggle of man against the powers
of nature, which at any moment might destroy
him and his work.*

An Introduction to Santorini

Santorini is one of the most southerly islands in the Cyclades. It lies between Ios and Anafi, has an area of 96 square kilometres and a permanent population of 11,381. It is situated 130 nautical miles from Piraeus, 70 nautical miles from Crete and has a coastline 69 kilometres long.

It has a pleasant climate and rather cool summers. The temperatures remain fairly low thanks to the prevailing northeast winds that blow through the region.

Fira is the capital, Athinios the main port.

The west coast of Santorini ends in a steep precipice and is lost in the caldera, the circular lagoon-like body of water that measures 32 square miles and is 300 to 400 metres deep.

To the west the caldera is rimmed by Therasia and the uninhabited, much smaller islet of Aspronisi.

From the placement of thise islands it is easy to imagine the outline of another, larger island.

In the cliffs surrounding the caldera, which range in height from 150 to 300 metres, the horizontal, parallel bands of red and black rock and lava that were formed during repeated eruptions, constitute a unique cross-section in the earth for those who wish to study the island's distant past.

Perched on the rim of the cliffs are the island's main towns, Fira and Ia.

The landscape of the outer side of Santorini is very different from the cliffs overlooking the caldera.

The earth spreads out in terraces as far as the valley that extends gently down to the sea. This is the most fertile part of the island and where the other towns, Pyrgos and Emborio to the south, Karterado and Finikia to the north, are situated.

Here too is where Santorini's most popular beaches are found - Kamari, Perissa and Monolithos - all with pebbles or black sand.

This side of Santorini has its limestone outcroppings and hills, though: Prophitis Elias, Gavrilos, Monolithos, Mikros Prophitis Elias and Megalo Vouno. The highest peak, Prophitis Elias, does not exceed 556 metres.

From its northern tip, Cape Mavropetra, to its southern tip, Cape Exomytis, the island measures 18 kilometres. It width varies from 2 to 6 kilometres. Santorini

owes its unique topography and its elliptical shape to volcanic activity in the prehistoric era.

The island's soil, thanks to its origins, is particularly fertile. From early on, it was famous for its produce. Because it could not support large quantities of fruit and vegetables, due to the lack of water, whatever did manage to grow was especially succulent. Among the most prized of these products was its wine. Apart from the brusco and vinsanto vintages, Santorini also brought forth a variety called "nychteri", a name derived from the way in which it was made. It was a wine made from unpressed grapes, those that had been picked at the end of the day and lay in mounds waiting to be crushed the next morning. The juice would seep from them very slowly, squeezed out by their own weight.

Apart from vines, the island also favours tomatoes, small perhaps but exceptionally tasty. The locals made tomato paste from them to store for the difficult days of winter. They also grew barley, cucumbers and yellow peas, "the most delicious peas ever known".

They came from a special variety of pulse cultivated on the island.

The locals used to puree the dried peas with a stone handmill, boil them with a little oil, and then serve them cold as a "meze" sprinkled with more oil and some chopped onions.

When someone wanted to boast about his peas or "fava", he used to say they came from Santorini.

Another of the island's important economic resources was the pumice deposits that extend along the surface of its soil, at some points reaching up to 30 to 40 metres thick.

Large quantities of this material, which has insulatory properties, were used in the construction of the Suez Canal.

Today the islanders are mostly engaged in professions related to tourism.

The only traditional occupation they still follow is cultivating the vineyards to make wine.

The tomato-processing plants stand abandoned, silent remnants of the past, while the donkeys that used to go up and down the island laden with baskets brimful of vegetables now transport the countless visitors from Kato Yialo up to Fira.

Santorini in recent years has developed into a summer holiday resort for thousands of Greeks and foreigners. Its important archaeological sites and its stunning beauty, which is mainly a function of its extraordinary landscape, attract thousands of tourists from all over the world every summer.

▲ Dozens of churches lie scattered in every corner of Santorini, proof of the islanders' deep religious faith.

► The slope of the land forced the local builders to make unusual connections: here the terrace of one house forms the roof of the one below.

► The sheer sides of the caldera vanish abruptly into the sea, reminding us of the prehistoric disaster.

Myth and History

VOLCANIC ACTIVITY

Over the centuries, the islanders have given their home various names. It has been called Strongyle (the Round One), Kalliste (the Beautiful One), Philotera, and Santorini.

In the 20th century, many people have linked its turbulent past with the tragic fate of the legendary continent of Atlantis.

Scholars and scientists, geologists and archaeologists, have treated it with wonder and interest as they tried to piece together its long story from the information available to them. But let's see how its tragic history unfolds. Mythology tells us that Santorini was created from a lump of earth from far-off Libya.

History, complemented by geology and archaeology, gives us a series of mind-shattering facts related to the creation and evolution of this amazing place, which the French geologist, F. Fouque, rightly calls the "Pompeii of the Aegean".

But in order for us to follow Santorini's progress through the ages, we should first try to sketch a picture of what Greece looked like hundreds of millions of years ago.

In the beginning, the Greek earth was covered by water. Gradually and after cosmogonic upheavals in the bowels of the planet, sections of dry land rose up above the water some 30,000,000 years ago and created Aigaiida or Aigeida. Aigaiida was a single land mass that stretched from the Ionian Sea to Asia Minor and the south coast of Crete. The geological shifts in the earth's crust continued. With the passage of time, the sea penetrated the interior of Aigaiida breaking it into pieces. Part of it, what is today covered by the Aegean Sea, sank, leaving only its mountain peaks which still protrude above the surface. In the place now occupied by Santorini a rocky islet had remained, at what corresponds today to the district of Prophitis Elias and Pyrgos.

From this time on, the subsequent evolution of the island into its present shape was the result of the long-term activity of volcanoes, which had appeared in the region as early as 26,000,000 years or so before.

Thus, about 2,000,000 years ago, the first volcanic craters began to be formed southwest of Prophitis Elias, Over time, the craters broke through the surface of

the sea and then united to form what is now Akrotiri. Later volcanic activity would create other craters to the north of the already existing island. The volcanic cones and the rocky islet predating them slowly began to unite, due to the matter that spilled out during eruptions, eventually forming a single island, which because of its shape was called, as Herodotus tells us, Strongyle or the Round One. What did Strongyle really look like, one wonders, in those days?

Scientists have concluded that it must have been an imposing volcanic cone, with a height of about 1,000 metres and a diameter of 14 to 15 kilometres. There must have been a crater at the top of the cone and other smaller ones along its sides. Lava would have burst from the craters, to flow bubbling hot down to the sea.

With time the volcano became extinct and after thousands of years plants and animals began to live on the island. Its fertile soil must have attracted the first colonists, as finds (pottery and idols) from the archaeological digs indicate, around 3000 B.C., i.e. during the second Early Cycladic period. They must have belonged to a tribe called the Lelegians, who were the first settlers on the other Cyclades, as well. The excavations at Akrotiri verify the existence of an important civilization during the next period, the Middle Cycladic, from 2000/1900 to 1550 B.C. on Santorini and Therasia. By then, these first inhabitants had founded a settlement, which in the years that followed underwent considerable development.

Apart from being farmers, they, like the inhabitants of the other Cycladic islands at this time, must have been awesome sailors.

In the succeeding years. when Minoan Crete had become a maritime empire, Cretans came to settle on the island and intermarried with the locals.

Around 1550-1500 B.C., this civilization was suddenly terminated, while it was at its peak.

The cause was the violent eruption of the volcano, during which as we shall see, a large portion of the island exploded and sank to the bottom of the sea.

THE CHRONICLE OF THE CATASTROPHE

Let's go back to 1550-1500 B.C., the middle of the 16th century B.C. Written documents, which could tell us exactly what happened, do not exist. Historians try, from other evidence within their grasp, to piece together the picture of that dreadful catastrophe that befell Santorini. Earthquakes were always a common occurrence in the region. One especially catastrophic earthquake triggered the awakening of the volcano this time. The houses, two- and three-storey, were partially destroyed. Most of the residents abandoned the island in panic. And it appears that, forewarned by some worrying sign, they did not return. They took whatever valuables they had with them. The digs at Akrotiri have unearthed no objects of any worth, jewels, seals or other valuables, no skeletons of humans or animals, apart from that of a pig. Today, one can see traces of heavy objects having been moved imprinted on the ash and pumice. This tells us that some of the inhabitants must have stayed on the island until the volcano started to erupt. Even these people, however, since their skeletons have not been found, must have left Thera at some point. Spyros Marinatos, who was in charge of the excavations at Akrotiri, called these people troglodytes, people who lived among the ruins. Christos Doumas, the archaeologist who succeeded Marinatos, believes that they formed a team who were attempting to repair the damaged buildings. The amount of time that elapsed between the earthquake and the eruption of the volcano is not known. However, it must have been at least a year. Scientists have deduced this from the fact that some seeds left in the ruined houses after the earthquake had begun to sprout when the first ash started to fall from the erupting volcano.

The whole island was buried under a thick layer of pumice, which at many points is over thirty metres deep. Huge chunks of basalt were thrown from the crater with such force that many of the houses at Akrotiri were struck by them. The intensity of the explosion must have been tremendous. The descriptions that have come down to us of later, smaller eruptions can help us a bit to imagine what this nightmare must have been like. Foreign travellers in more modern times, who happened to be on the island during the eruptions of 1657 and 1707, vividly describe the frightening turmoil of nature, the atmosphere, the fear and panic of the residents at this disaster, which could put them from moment to moment at the mercy of unleashed natural forces. The fury of the volcano was always accompanied by strong tremors from the earth, which made "... the houses rock from side to side like babies' cradles, to bend like reeds blown by the wind." Flames burst forth shrouded with thick clouds, smoke "...rose up from the flaming abyss towards the heights", and thick sulphurous steam billowed up like black clouds. Lightning forged furrows in the sky, thunder claps and strong explosions were heard, while the air smelled foul. The sea was seething, changing colour constantly, from deep green to reddish and later a bright yellow. White ash like chalk or burnt plaster was ejected with such force that it did not fall to earth till it reached Asia Minor. The loud thunder was accompanied by enormous rocks that were hurled as much as three miles from the crater. All the gold and silver possessions of the locals turned black, the islanders suffered terrible pains in their eyes and were unable to see for two or three days afterwards, while many animals were asphyxiated by the polluted air.

Something similar, though far more intense, must have occurred on those long ago days between 1550 and 1500 B.C.

The material that was thrown up from inside the cone of the volcano, which is in the centre of the island, appears to have created a huge vacuum inside. The crust of the earth receded and the larger central portion of Strongyle, after blowing up, was sucked down into that vacuum.

Eighty-three square kilometres of earth vanished into the abyss of the crater which, at the time of its creation, had a depth of 800 m.

The sea rushed in and flooded the spot, which had once been dry land. All that remains of Strongyle today is Santorini, Therasia and Aspronisi. This catastrophe of truly Biblical proportions must have been accompanied by enormous tidal waves which, according to the experts, could have reached a height of 210 metres at the start before slamming against the shores of Aegean with indescribable fury. The three-day night of Heracles and myths from Attica, the Argolid, the Aegean islands and Lycia are probably nothing more than tales from the memories of people who had lived through this incredible disaster and who were attempting to wrest some meaning out of the ensuing phenomena.

For a series of days darkness must have reigned and day was turned into night. The volcanic ash that spewed forth must have fallen on the earth within a huge circumference, charring all vegetation. The residents of the affected areas must have suffered from bronchitis, eye trouble, skin diseases and intestinal problems.

As a means of understanding the dimensions of the catastrophes that occurred in that far-off year and their consequences, we can look at the 1883 eruption of Krakatoa, in the strait of Sounda between Java and Sumatra. In that eruption, 22.8 square kilometres of the island were blown up and then sank to a depth of 200-300 metres. Witnesses' reports are mind boggling, the scale of the disaster inconceivable. For several months the ports near Krakatoa were unapproachable by ships. Ash covered the sky for a distance of 150 kilometres. The noise of the explosions was heard 2 kilometres away; they caused tidal waves 30 metres in height, which flooded several regions on Sumatra with a vengeance and swept away an entire city on nearby Java. An estimated 30,000 people were killed. Having this information in mind, we can perhaps form a picture, albeit blurred, of what happened when prehistoric Strongyle blew up in what was, as far as we know, the most violent explosion in the history of the earth.

The crater which was created after the eruption was four times the size and depth of that of the island of Krakatoa. The phenomena that accompanied the explosions and sinking of the cone of the volcano and the finding of pumice during his excavations at Amnissos in Crete in 1932, led Professor Spyros Marinatos to formulate the following theory:

The decline of the Minoan civilization around 1500 B.C. was not the result of enemy invasion but of the blow dealt by the frightful consequences of the eruption of the volcano on Santorini. The tidal waves must literally have shaved the shores of Crete, where not only the palace of Knossos stood, but also those of Mallia, Zakros, Amnissos, Nirou Hani and the large village of Gournia. The interior of the island must have been badly damaged by the strong seismic tremors which shook the whole region.

This theory has not been accepted unreservedly because the dating of samples of Minoan pottery places the decline of Minoan civilization at least fifty years after the eruption at Santorini. For many scholars, this means that the Minoans were brought down by foreign conquerors, most probably the Achaeans.

Nevertheless, what is considered almost certain is that the effect of the eruption of the Thera volcano on all of the Aegean, including Crete, must have been horrendous.

ATLANTIS QUESTION

Santorini has often been connected with Atlantis, the legendary continent that sank to the bottom of the sea while it was at its zenith. The mystery surrounding the destruction of the one and the disappearance of the other has preoccupied scientists for generations. References to the civilization of Atlantis are found in Plato's dialogues, "Timaeus" and "Critias".

The myth of Atlantis was first told to Solon by the Egyptian priests of Saida, when the Athenian lawgiver visited their country in 590 B.C. Solon then related it to Dropis, the father of Critias's great-grandfather.

In discussing Atlantis, Plato mentions that "it was a large and wonderful state superior to the other islands". It owed its supremacy to the remarkable civilization it had nurtured. It was a kingdom composed of two islands, the "greater" and the "lesser", which in turn consisted of ten states. Of these, only two are alluded to by name, the "Metropolis" and the "Royal State". Their boundaries included part of Libya up to Egypt and part of Europe as far as Tyrrhenia.

At some point, Atlantis tried to conquer Egypt and Attica. But the Athenians, as the leaders of the Greeks, successfully resisted invasion and put them to flight. It was precisely at this time that huge floods and powerful earthquakes struck Atlantis causing it to vanish taking with it the Athenian soldiers. These events, as we are told, must have occurred some 900 years before Solon's rule or, in other words, in about 1500 B.C., when the Santorini volcano is thought to have erupted.

The finds from the digs at Akrotiri, which indicate the presence of a high level of civilization, its violent cessation, and the synchronicity in the dates of the two catastrophes have led many scholars to conclude that the lost Atlantis was none other than Santorini.

Spyros Marinatos' interpretation of the

myth seems more logical. According to him, the identification of Minoan Crete with Atlantis is very probable, since the disasters that beset Crete after the eruption were fatal to its further development. The topography and shape of Atlantis, as described by the ancients, greatly resemble those of the valley of Messara in Heraklion prefecture. Crete could well have been the "greater" island, the "Royal State", while Santorini, with which Crete had ties, would have been the "Metropolis" or "lesser" island.

Over the centuries, as the myth was told and retold, it is very likely that the events underwent subtle changes. Thus the destruction of a civilization, the Minoan, was attributed to the vanishing of the island. The island that was blown up and subsequently sank was not Crete, however, but rather a large portion of Santorini.

Nevertheless, the question still remains. Was there an Atlantis?

Or did Plato, perhaps wishing to instruct his compatriots on the consequences that can arise when mortals are lacking in respect for the gods, himself fabricate the myth of the lost continent drawing on tales about the real destruction of Santorini?

A BRIEF OVERVIEW OF THE ISLAND'S HISTORY FROM 1300 B.C. TO MORE MODERN TIMES

After the eruption of the volcano between 1550 and 1500 B.C., the island remained uninhabited for about two centuries. Traces of human life have been found, dating to the late 13th century B.C. According to Herodotus, the Phoenicians were so enthralled by the beauty of Santorini that they settled there and gave it the name Kalliste (which means beautiful).

Tradition maintains that Santorini was colonized by Membliaros together with some of Cadmus's men, when the Phoenician king was searching for his sister, Europa, who had been abducted by Zeus in the guise of a bull.

Tradition also relates that later the Minyans from Boeotia established a settlement on Thera. Herodotus, however, informs us that at the end of the 12th century B.C., around 1115 B.C., the Dorians arrived from Sparta, led by King Theras, who was the son of Autesion, grandson of Cadmus and a descendant of Oedipus. Although he was a Theban hero, Theras lived in Sparta as viceroy and guardian of his young nephews, Procles and Eurysthenes. When the latter came of age, Theras left Sparta and thus arrived in Santorini, where he settled. Ever after, the island was called Thera in his honour.

By the 9th century B.C., it was a thoroughly Dorian colony, whose centre was at Ancient Thera on a fortified position on Mesa Vouno (Middle Mountain). During this time, Santorini, along with the shores of southeastern mainland Greece, Crete, Milos and Cyprus, constituted a bridge unifying East and West. True descendants of the Spartans, the Therans had created a closed society which permitted but few influences from outside, and those only from residents of neighbouring islands. However, the location they had chosen was so crucial to sea communication that, although they did not follow the rest of the Cyclades in their development, they nevertheless could not remain completely unaffected by what was going on around them.

Thus, by the late 9th or early 8th century B.C., i.e. around 825 B.C., Thera led Crete and Milos in adopting the Phoenician alphabet to the written Greek language. In the 7th and 6th century B.C., the island began to have contact with other regions of Greece, such as Crete and Paros initially, and later with Attica, Corinth, Rhodes and Ionia in Asia Minor.

► *The volcano's fury created strange shapes, such as "Bear Rock".*

Its inhabitants subsisted on a frugal diet, consisting solely of what the island could produce. They were concerned with neither trade nor navigation.

The first people to leave the island did so in 630 B.C., founding a colony on the north coast of Africa called Cyrrhene. They only resorted to this after a long period of drought, which scourged the island for seven years.

By the 6th century B.C. Thera was minting its own currency.

During the Classical era (5th and 4th century B.C.), it continued to remain on the sidelines. It was subjugated by the Persians and the mint ceased functioning. During the Peloponnesian War Thera allied itself with the Spartans. In 426/425 B.C. it came under the control of the Athenians and was forced to join the Delian League. When the Macedonians gained supremacy over the rest of Greece, Thera too followed. Likewise, during the Hellenistic period, it was ruled by the Ptolemies of Egypt, who valued its strategic location enough to found the harbour of Eleusina there. They also transformed the Mesa Vouno district, and Ancient Thera, into a major base for the military operations they were conducting in the Aegean.

Under Roman domination, from 146 B.C., Thera fell into total obscurity. Within the vast sphere of Roman influence it was nothing more than one of a dozen other inconsequential Aegean islands. During the Byzantine era, it acquired a modicum of political and military significance. It was incorporated into the Byzantine empire and belonged to the Theme of the Aegean. Christianity must have reached Thera in the 3rd century. By the end of that century there were already converts to the new religion on the island.

By the start of the 4th century it had an organized church, which is referred to as the Bishopric of Thera, the first bishop having been Dioskouros (342-344). It was one of eleven bishoprics that were subject to the Cathedral of Rhodes and ranked fifth. The prosperity of the Christian community on Thera in the early Christian era is borne out by the existence of three old basilicas. One of them was erected at Ancient Thera on Mesa Vouno and must have been dedicated to the Archangel Michael. The second was built on the site of the present Byzantine church of Piskopi at Gonia. It was on its ruins that the emperor Alexios I Komninos founded the Panayia of Gonia or Our Lady of Piskopi in 1081-1118, perhaps as a Catholic monastery. The third basilica was erected at Perissa where the Byzantine church of Ayia Irini stands today.

In 1153, for the first time, we find mention of the island in the writings of the Arab geographer Edris under a new name, Santorini. It seems to have been called that by the Crusaders, after the chapel of Ayia Irini (Santa Irini - Santorini), which some scholars place at Perissos, others on Therasia.

With the taking of Constantinople by the

Crusaders in 1204, Santorini passed into the hands of Marco Sanudo, along with many of the other islands in the Aegean, in 1207. It thus became a part of the Duchy of Naxos or of the Archipelago. Sanudo then ceded Santorini together with Therasia as a barony to Giacomo Barozzi. The Orthodox bishop was expelled from the island, a Roman Catholic installed instead. His seat was one of the four Latin bishoprics of the Duchy. The island's capital was moved to the castle of Skaros. The Barozzi family governed Santorini until 1335. With their expulsion the barony of Santorini reverted to the Duchy of Naxos. Under this new period of Sanudo hegemony, the cultivation of cotton began to progress. From 1397 to 1418, Santorini was governed by Duke Giacomo Crispo. In 1480 the Duke of Naxos, Giacomo III Crispo, gave his daughter in marriage to the Duke of Candia (Crete), Domenico Pisani, with Santorini as her dowry. After the death of Giacomo, however, his brother laid claim to the island and after some dispute it was recognized as belonging to the Duchy of Naxos.

In 1487, Santorini and the other islands in the Duchy were annexed by Venice. The Latins, during their occupation of Greece as well as afterwards, attempted to strengthen their position by installing Jesuit missionaries on the island and by encouraging the conversion of as many inhabitants as possible to the Catholic faith. At the same time, the Orthodox faction was endeavouring to keep their language and faith alive through the founding of schools and churches. Under the Latins, Santorini like the rest of the islands was a victim of the rivalry among local leaders as well as of repeated looting by pirates, who had already become the scourge of the Aegean in the days of Byzantium. For defensive purposes, therefore, five settlements were created within

▼ *The Byzantine church of (E)Piskopi at Gonia.*

fortresses in the interior of the island: Skaros, the most important; Epanomeria (Epano Meros - Ia); Pyrgos, erected during the Byzantine era; Nimborio; and Akrotiri. In 1537, Khaireddin Barbarossa captured Santorini on behalf of the Sultan. With the ousting of the Latins, the Orthodox Bishopric of Santorini was reinstated. Nevertheless, the island continued to be governed, even if in name only, until 1566 by the Crispi dynasty. After the definitive removal of the Crispi, Santorini was ceded by the Sublime Porte to Joseph Nazi, a Jew, who governed it for a short time until it was subjugated by the Turks in 1579. The Turks did not settle on the island. They merely renamed it Deitmetzik, or Small Mill, because of the many windmills there. During the Turkish occupation, the islanders enjoyed relative autonomy. In exchange for this privilege, they were obliged to pay a tax both to the Sultan and to La Serenissma, the Republic of Venice. The Orthodox Bishopric was elevated to an Archbishopric. The island was subject to the so-called Urban Code of Santorini, which seems to have been derived from Byzantine law. It was governed by Elders who were elected by the inhabitants and who in turn represented them before the Ottoman authorities. Every other year the Kadis came to the island to dispense justice. Piracy died down, making it possible for navigation to develop. Santorini gradually acquired its own distinguished fleet. Trade and transport grew, facilitating the promotion of local products, such as its celebrated wine and cotton. Santorini opened relations with all the major ports in the Eastern Mediterranean. One indication of the prosperity that reigned during those days is the fact that in 1780 the monastery of Prophitis Elias possessed its own ship. In addition, there were two shipbuilding yards at Armeni in the Epanomeria district and at Athinios, not to mention the impressive mansions being built in the villages, which can be seen even today. In the meantime, by the end of the 17th century, the class composed of descendants of the Latin conquerors had begun to decline, and as a result there was a considerable drop in the number of Catholics on the island. Shipping and trade continued to flourish into the early 19th century. In 1821 with the outbreak of the Greek war of Independence, Santorini's fleet was the third largest in the country, after those of Hydra and Spetses. The emergence of the steamboat at the end of the 19th century brought an end to Santorini's shipping wealth, and the island's decline was tragically capped by the catastrophic earthquakes of 1956. Life was shattered. Most of the buildings were damaged, many collapsed completely. The event marked the start of the island's decay and abandonment, which continued into the 1970s. During this period, however, the interest of scientists, archaeologists, historians and geologists in Santorini's past began to lift it back to centre stage. As time goes by, more and more people are discovering it. Its reconstruction is well on its way and works are being undertaken to modernize its infrastructure. Today the past seems very remote. In summer this once ignored Aegean island resembles a buzzing beehive. For thousands of Greeks and foreigners it has become a favourite place to spend the whole summer, for others it's an ideal holiday spot.

Taking one last look at the past, we note that during the years between 1550/1500 B.C. and 1950, the volcano has shown signs of activity fourteen times to a greater or lesser degree. The first eruption occurred in 197/196 B.C. and resulted in the formation of Old Kammeni, called Iera or Holy by the ancients. In 1573 sections of dry land emerged successively to unite with Little Kammeni and to create the present volcano, Nea Kammeni.

► *Nea Kammeni consitsts of masses of petrified black lava.*

*T*he prehistoric town

The first inhabitants arrived on Strongyle around 3000 B.C. They created, as we have said, a prehistoric settlement, traces of which first came to light in 1860 in a mine on Therasia. Ten years later, the French archaeologists, H. Gorceix and H. Mamet, members of the French Archaeological School, at the instigation of their geologist compatriot, Fouque, who had worked on the eruptions of the Santorini volcano, began excavations at the mines of Therasia and subsequently in the area of Akrotiri on Thera itself. Later the efforts of the French team were continued by the German baron Hiller von Kartrinken, who while conducting excavations at Mesa Vouno in search of Ancient Thera also began digging around Akrotiri. Systematic research at Akrotiri to locate the prehistoric settlement did not begin until 1967 under the supervision of the distinguished Greek archaeologist, Spyros Marinatos. Then the digs revealed the Late Minoan city of Akrotiri, the centre of a major Aegean civilization of the mid 16th century B.C. This centre, although influenced significantly by Crete, the dominant power in the region at the time, nevertheless managed to retain its own characteristic features.

The wealth and quality of the houses which have been discovered to date demonstrate that Akrotiri was a flourishing city. The inhabitants led a comfortable and refined life, reminiscent of Minoan Crete, while the architecture of the city contains strong Cycladic elements. The buildings were two - or three - storeys high with many rooms. The most luxurious were constructed of fitted stone (which is why the archaeologists call them "xestes" [scraped]); the others were made of mud mixed with straw. The ground floor communicated with the upper floors by a wooden or stone interior staircase. To reinforce the buildings against earthquake tremors - let's not forget that they were particularly common in the area - wooden frames were used, as they were in Crete. The floors of the houses were usually of tamped earth, often paved with uncut slabs of slate. This kind of floor was most commonly found in the antechambers and in the rooms on the upper storeys. In other floors, the earth was inlaid with pieces of seashell (as in room A2 and on the first floor of B6), or covered with a kind of pebble mosaic (as in room D8). The roofs must have been flat and strewn with earth for insulation, a technique prevalent in the Cyclades until a few years ago. The storerooms, workshops and grain mills were always located on the ground floor. If a space was used for food storage it would have small windows to offer better preservation conditions. If it contained a workshop, mill or shop, then the room would have a large window placed right next to the door. The spaces on the upper floors were the residential rooms. Many of the walls were embellished with exquisite frescoes. According to Spyros Marinatos, the rooms with frescoes were special places reserved for worship. On the upper floor(s) the windows were large and the rooms filled with light. Looms were frequently found in them. The roads of the town were narrow and paved with flagstones. The drainage network consisted of built-in channels laid under the surface of the pavement. The sewage was led to the channels by clay pipes, which were incorporated in the walls of the houses.

► *The facade of West House, bordering the north side of Triangle Square.*

27

GUIDE TO THE ARCHAEOLOGICAL SITE AT AKROTIRI

◄ *The east side of Xeste 4.*

In 1932, while Spyros Marinatos was excavating at Amnissos on Crete, he was impressed by the violence with which a Minoan villa in the area had been destroyed. Then on the ground floor of another building, which lay closer to the sea, he noticed the presence of pumice.

These incidents, as we mentioned earlier, started him thinking that the human factor had not been the cause of the blows to the civilization of Crete and the subsequent dissolution of its economy.

It must have been something else, something far more powerful. He sought the answer to the question that arose in the eruption of the Santorini volcano in prehistoric times.

Thus, in 1967, several years after the publication in 1939 of his theory in a scholarly journal, he began excavating on Thera at Akrotiri. He chose this site over other possibilities as being the most suitable, firstly because it lay so close to the sea and directly opposite Crete — two features favourable to the development of an important prehistoric relationship. In addition, there were visible traces of sherds, pottery, and the like on the surface of the earth in the area. Furthermore, it was here that the most significant architectural remains had been found during digs undertaken in the past century by the French archaeologists H. Mamet and H. Gorceix.

The finds that came to light at Akrotiri belonged to a settlement which must have extended from north to south. The north part of the city must have sunk into the crater during the eruption. Up to now the excavations have revealed only one road of this settlement and the buildings below it. The road, which divided the city into north and south districts, has been called Telchinon street by the archaeologists.

We enter the covered part of the dig through the southern section of the prehistoric city.

On our left, the first building we come to is called Xeste 3. It is an impressive structure with at least three storeys and fourteen rooms on each floor. Its facade is made of fitted stone (ashlar masonry).

A staircase led to the first floor where many rooms were decorated with frescoes, such as the Crocus Gatherers.

In the south part of the building scattered stone tools were found. If we accept the theory that after the earthquake special teams remained behind on the island to repair the damaged buildings, then it is possible that these tools belonged to them.

As we step onto Telchinon street and follow it to the north, the first building we see on our left is building C. Its entrance is right on Telchinon street. Many stone tools were found here, too.

On our right, as we continue, we come to the two-storey building B. On the ground floor in room B1 a series of "pitharia" or large jars were found, resting in special niches. Next to them were scattered several cone-shaped funnels used for emptying the liquids. In room B2 on the same floor there were numerous cooking vessels and some cone-shaped cups. The walls of

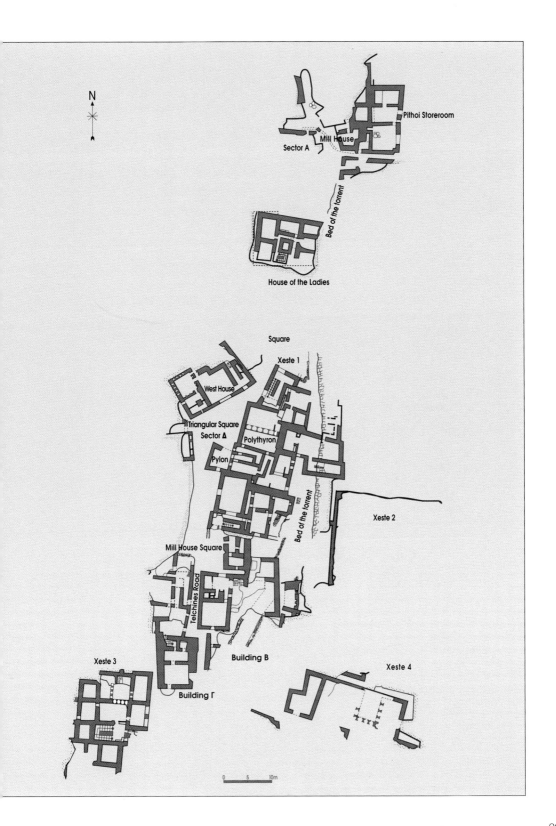

N

Pithoi Storeroom

Sector A   Mill House

Bed of the Torrent

House of the Ladies

Square

Xeste 1

West House

Triangular Square
Sector Δ
Polythyron

Pylon

Bed of the Torrent

Xeste 2

Mill House Square

Telchines Road

Xeste 3

Building B

Xeste 4

Building Γ

0   5   10m

the room above B1 were decorated with the frescoes of the Boxing Boys and the Antelopes.

Further along the road is the Miller's square. It is bordered to the south and east by building B and on the north by complex D. It takes its name from the flour mill that was found in room D15, directly opposite room B1. You can still see the mill and the jar in which the ground flour was collected.

Complex D has four entrances. One of them, the western one, was protected by a gate. Room D2 in the east wing of complex D was decorated with the frescoes of the Lilies and Spring. Traces of a bed and a footstool were discovered in the same place; a copy of the bed exists in the Archaeological Museum in Athens.

Passing through the gate, we find ourselves in Triangle square. It is larger than the previous square and is bordered on the east and south by complex D, on the west by another building and on the north by the so-called West House.

West House was originally decorated with the frescoes of the Young Priestess, the Fisherman, and all the miniatures except for that of the Monkeys.

As we leave West House, we can see that Telchinon street, beyond the north

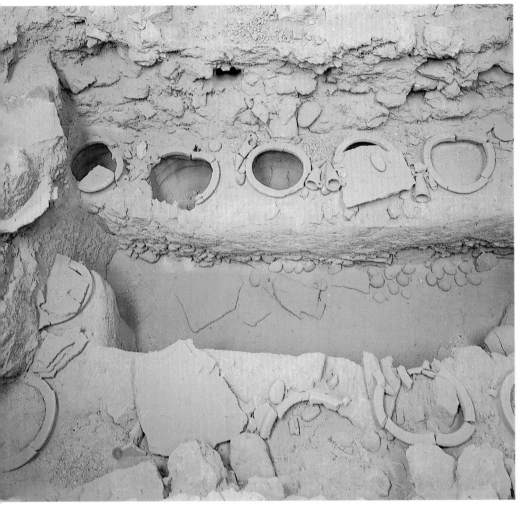

entrance to complex D, has been destroyed by the water from a stream. We continue walking northwards. Now Telchinon street is bordered on the west by the house of the Women. It was in the north wing of this building that the frescoes of the Women and the Papyruses were found. It also yielded pottery, stone utensils and tools, among which was a half-finished marble object, most probably a vase. We wind up our visit in section A, the point where the excavation began in 1967.
Three rooms in its northernmost section must have been storerooms, for many pitharia were found here.

1. The prehistoric inhabitants stored flour and barley in these huge jars.

2. A series of jars incorporated in the ledge on the ground floor of room 1 in Xeste 2.

Some of them still contained carbonized flour and barley. There are large windows in the walls of these rooms, through which the stored goods were most probably distributed.
The fragmentary fresco of the African was found in a room in this building.

ECONOMIC AND SOCIAL ORGANIZATION AT AKROTIRI

No written documents of any kind have been found in the prehistoric city of Akrotiri. This has meant that, in order to form any picture of the economic and social life there before the catastrophe, scientists have had to rely solely on the rich finds unearthed by the digs. Before discussing the theories on the social organization of Late Minoan Thera that have been formulated over time, let's first take a look at its economy. The most important sectors of the island's economy were farming, animal raising, fishing and navigation. This has been proven by the discovery of ancient jars filled with barley seeds, flour, and legumes, such as yellow peas and other vetches.

They also must have cultivated sesame seeds and practiced beekeeping, and were surely familiar with the olive, since so many amphoras — which were used primarily for transporting olive oil — have been brought to light. Bunches of grapes are often depicted on vases, revealing that vines were cultivated, too. This is borne out by the discovery of various jars which were used to store liquids.

The Akrotirians were also occupied with the collection of crocuses, which they used, along with the purple extracted from the murex shell, to dye cloth.

They raised sheep, goats and pigs and kept oxen as beasts of burden. Apart from being farmers and herdsmen, they were also fishermen. This has been deduced from the frescoes, such as the one of the Fisherman, and from the fossilized fishbones and seashells found amongst the ruins and in amphoras.

The reputation of the Cycladic islanders as seafarers as well as scenes in the frescoes, such as that of the Fleet, lead to the conclusion that the citizens of Akrotiri must have had a well developed merchant navy.

This would have permitted them to maintain trade with Crete and mainland Greece, as indeed is shown in the influences that have been detected and the presence of foreign pottery at the site. The depiction in their frescoes of subjects that are not native to Greece but rather related to the landscape of Egypt indicates that they also had contact with that region. Furthermore, the discovery of a Syrian amphora shows that Akrotiri must have had some dealings with the peoples of the Eastern Mediterranean, as well.

The presence of looms in many of the houses demonstrates that the women were often occupied with weaving. Moreover, the large number of vases and other types of pottery tells us that another flourishing sector of the economy was that of ceramic production.

In addition, the finding of stone tools and vessels, such as mills, pestles, hammers and the like, implies the development of masonry.

Finally, the quality of the town planning, architecture and painting at Akrotiri shows that the Santorinians of that period were superb builders, engineers, masons and artists.

At the same time, the architecture and the layout of the settlement at Akrotiri reveal0 a good deal about the structure of its society.

The theories that have emerged over the years about this society can be summarized as follows:

To begin with, the kinds of spaces that existed in each building and their location (with the workshops and storerooms on the ground floor and the living quarters upstairs) lead us to the conclusion that each house lent a certain degree of self-sufficiency to its occupants.

In addition, the fact that up to now more than one large, comfortable house has been excavated shows that the wealth of the area was not concentrated in the hands of a single family.

Furthermore, no palace has yet been found; therefore, there may not have been a ruler. This conclusion is confirmed by the town's layout and its architecture, which also indicate that power was not exercised by one person, but by many.

These observations have given rise to the theory that Akrotiri society was governed by the priestly class, which also controlled the economy.

Also, the failure to unearth any temple convinced professor Spyros Marinatos that each house must have contained its own private place of worship. He formulated the idea that the Akrotirians must have worshipped nature and fertility, as was the case in neighbouring Crete.

He maintained that the large individual buildings must have been the residences of important officials and that Xeste 3 was the religious and administrative centre of the community. What, however, was the relationship between Late Minoan Thera and Crete?

From all that we have already said, it is obvious that Akrotiri was self-sufficient economically.

Although it was influenced by Minoan Crete in terms of architecture and the arts, its culture was entirely its own. Consequently, Akrotiri cannot be thought of as a Minoan colony. To the contrary, Cretans must have taken up residence here to exploit the economic possibilities of the island and its occupants. In other words, it was a kind of trading station for Crete.

POTTERY

◀ 1. Tall, narrow vase with swallows (Athens, National Archaeological Museum).

▼ 2. This ethmos or colander was a typical example of the pottery found in the prehistoric city (Athens, National Archaeological Museum).

▼ 3. So-called breast pitcher with swallows (Athens, National Archaeological Museum).

► 4. Ewer with swallow decoration (Athens, National Archaeol. Museum).

As we have said, pottery as an art and as an economic activity was especially highly developed at Akrotiri.
The excavations have revealed two types of pots: those which were made on the island and those which were imported from other places, such as the Argolid and particularly Crete.
In all, fifty different shapes have been discovered. Many of the vessels have a religious character, such as the rhytons (cup shaped like a horn or an animal's head) and the tables on which offerings to the gods were placed.
The imported pottery was of extremely fine quality whose decoration varied depending on where it originated.
The pieces were generally small, being easier to transport. Conversely, the locally made pottery shows extreme diversity in size; it can be separated into objects for everyday use and luxury, decorative pieces.
The size of the common vessels differs according to their function.
The luxury objects are generally small, and made and decorated with greater care. The local pots were fashioned of whitish clay and decorated with dark designs, sometimes abstract patterns, sometimes motifs inspired by the plant and animal kingdom.
The painting on the pots was done freely, not confined to horizontal bands.
Typical examples of the pottery of Akrotiri are the sieve, the cylindrical flowerpot, and the so-called "breast jugs" (pitchers with breasts). These are thought to have had some ceremonial function; they could have been used for libations at fertility rites.

PAINTING

The art that was most highly developed at prehistoric Akrotiri was painting. This is immediately evident in the several marvellous frescoes that have been discovered up to now. These frescoes are not only genuine masterpieces in themselves, they also constitute invaluable sources for scholars seeking information on how people lived in that period.

Although the frescoes of Thera are reminiscent of those at Knossos, the artist's technique and mode of expression differ. And the technique is truly that of a "fresco", i.e. the subject is depicted on a moist surface, but with this important difference: The artist from Thera started to paint when the surface was still damp. As it dried, he continued working and by the time he finished, the surface was completely dry.

The paints he used were cream for the background, azure, black, yellow and red for the subject matter.

Before he began to work, he had to prepare the wall by smoothing the surface with pebbles he had collected from the sea for precisely that purpose.

The size of the surfaces covered by wall paintings varied, from small bands to large expanses of wall or pilasters of doors and windows.

The subjects portrayed, many of which are of a religious character, also displayed great variety: landscapes and scenes inspired by nature, scenes with people, compositions depicting some real event, such as the miniature showing the fleet, and, finally, purely decorative motifs, such as rosettes and rhomboid shapes.

A characteristic feature of the Thera wall paintings, apart from their vivid naturalism, is the freedom with which the subjects have been conceived and the expression of the artist. The works show such fidelity and freedom of movement that they come very close to being real portraits. This leads one to the conclusion that the painter was

not creating solely from his own imagination but that the subjects he was reproducing were familiar to him. Today, thousands of years later, the beauty of the Akrotiri frescoes continues to move us, unabated. They are all on exhibit at the Archaeological Museum in Athens and are described below.

The frieze with the **miniature of the monkeys** and the composition with the **Crocus Gatherers** from Xeste 3.

2. Fresco of the Young Priestess from room 1 of the Women's House (Athens, National Archaeological Museum).

3. The Papyrus fresco from room 1 of the Women's House (Athens, National Archaeological Museum).

The fresco of **the Antelopes** from room 1 of complex B. Depicting a pair of antelope facing each other framed by a sprig of ivy. They are of the Oryx Beissa species found in East Africa and are a popular subject in Egyptian

art of all periods. Here the figures of the animals have been rendered with simple, black outlines without recourse to many interior lines, the only exception being the heads, where certain details are shown with red highlights. The result is very impressive. The artist manages with the simplest of means to give his subject unbelievable precision and vitality.

The fresco of the **boys boxing** from

the south wall of the same room. The boys, each of whom wears a boxing glove on his right hand, are trying with great seriousness to avoid one another's blows. The composition skilfully conjures up the intensity and the effort of the small pugilists. On their heads they must have worn blue wigs, under which their own long black curly locks can be seen. This was the usual hairdo of the Minoans. The boy on the left of the fresco is wearing

more jewelry than his companion, a blue necklace, bracelets and an earring.
The fresco of the **monkeys** from room 6 of the same complex. Depicting lively monkeys climbing up some rocks, evidently because they are being chased. The last one, who must be the leader of the band, is turning his head towards the pursuers. This wall painting, too, although only a fragment survives, is full of vitality and

movement.
The fresco of **Spring** from room 2 of

▲ 1. Miniature of the Fleet or Parade of Ships found on the first floor, south side, of room 5 in West House (Athens, National Archaeological Museum).

▼ 2. Miniature from the north wall of room 5, West House.

▼ 3. The Spring fresco from room 2 of Xeste 4 (Athens, National Archaeological Museum).

complex D. This is the only wall painting in the Aegean that has been found intact. It covered three of the four walls in the room. It portrays a rocky landscape with red lilies. The rocks, some yellow, others green or red, have curious shapes like those seen in volcanic areas. From amongst them triple lilies protrude, looking as though they are blowing in the Aegean breeze. These triple lilies are also found in wall paintings in Crete, but there they are depicted with strict symmetry. Here, above the lilies swallows dart, as if in some courtship ritual. The presence of the swallows indicates that the season is spring. For scholars, geologists and volcano experts, this fresco holds enormous interest for it shows what Santorini looked like before the eruption, something totally unanticipated.

The fresco of the **Young Priestess** from room 4 in the fresco-covered West House. The woman appears to be holding an incenser with lit charcoal and is wearing a heavy, perhaps woollen, chiton.

The frescoes of the **Fishermen**, covering two corners of room 5 in the West House. They are each over 1 metre high. The men proudly show off their catch, the fish tied through the gills with a string.

The miniature of **the Fleet or the Parade of Ships**. This fresco is of considerable historical interest, because it is a rich source of information about life in the Aegean in the mid or late 16th century B.C. It covered the frieze above the windows of the south wall of the same room. This painting portrays the arrival or departure of a fleet, in full regalia, sailing to or from from one harbour on the left side to another on the right. One of the ships must have been the flagship. The many flags and the presence of the residents, some of whom seem to be waving goodbye

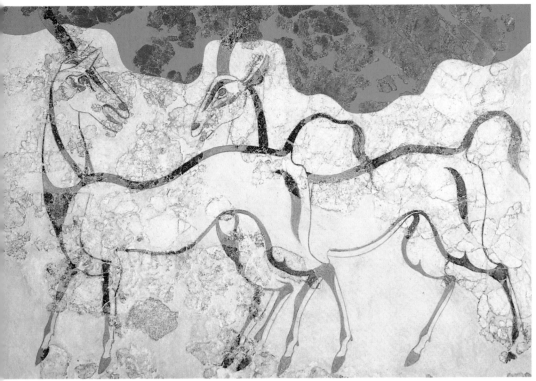

while others wave in greeting, intensifies the festive atmosphere of the scene. The helmets strung from the masts of the sailing ships tells us that the passengers are warriors. The houses shown in the painting are multi-storeyed, constructed of fitted ashlar masonry and arranged on different levels, very similar to those that have been unearthed at Akrotiri. But more than just giving us architectural clues, the fresco is a mine of information about the animals and plants in the area, the clothes people wore, shipbuilding techniques and the way the various parts of the ship functioned in prehistoric times. The scene depicted in this painting most probably refers to a specific historical event.

The miniature of **the River or Semitropical Landscape**. This covered the band that divided the eastern wall of the above mentioned room. Some scene unfolded around the river with figures of heroes, wild animals and birds. The north wall of the same room had a miniature which was executed on three levels: the first portrayed a naval battle, the second some warriors holding long spears and wearing shields and helmets, the third a pastoral scene. The fresco of the **Women** from room 1 of the House of the Women. The figures are dignified, with rouged cheeks and wearing jewelry. Finally, the fresco of the **Papyruses** from the same room in the House of the Women.

◄ 1. Stepped street in Ancient Thera with the House of the Phallus next to it.

► 2. The Roman theatre, built during the 3rd century B.C. under the Ptolemies.

Ancient Thera

The second important period in the history of Santorini is linked with the city of Ancient Thera. The excavations there, which began in 1896 by Baron Hiller von Gaertrinken in the area of Mesa Vouno, revealed ruins of a town which bore evidence of settlement as early as the 9th century B.C. The mountain of Prophitis Elias, Santorini's highest peak, runs eastward into the lower rocky outcropping of Mesa Vouno. These two mountains are joined by a ridge named Sellada. Mesa Vouno, with an altitude of 369 metres, extends from west to south and its steep slopes descend to the shore at Kamari to the north and at Perissos to the south. This naturally fortified spot was an ideal place for the Spartan colonists to found their city, and they built two roads, one to the beach at Kamari, where they had their port, ancient Ia, and the other to Perissos (or Perissa). The strategic location of the town was appreciated later by the Ptolemies. In the 4th century B.C., the most important era in the history of the island, Ancient Thera was transformed into an Egyptian naval base with the installation there of a major military guard post. Digs in the area have brought to light a settlement that stretched from northwest to southeast. It

was about 800 metres long and its greatest width was 150 metres. It was split in two by a central street, from which many side streets branched off. Because of the sloping terrain, many of the alleyways were stepped. All the streets were paved with flagstones, while sewage was conducted away via a system of covered channels. Of the buildings that have been discovered, the public ones were constructed of ashlar limestone blocks, a material found in abundance on the island, while private houses were made of small stones of irregular shape. The public buildings and the sanctuaries lie to the right and left of the main street. The private houses are clustered in two neighbourhoods, one of which ascends the west side of the mountain, the other the east. The layout of Ancient Thera as revealed by the digs is the form it acquired in the Hellenistic era. The excavations have also brought to light two cemeteries, one on the southwest slope of Sellada, the other under the rocks of Mesa Vouno. Both were in use during the Geometric period and up to the mid 7th century B.C. The cemetery used in the 6th, 5th and 4th centuries B.C. is located on the northeast slope of Sellada. The older graves, as a rule, are to be found at

higher points than the later ones. Observing the same burial rites as the Dorians of Kimolos and Crete, the Therans used to cremate their dead. They would put the ashes in a special funerary urn made for the purpose and then place the urn along with libations inside the family tomb. In some cases, however, the corpse was simply buried without being cremated.

GUIDE TO THE ARCHAEOLOGICAL SITE OF ANCIENT THERA

The entrance to the archaeological site of Ancient Thera is from the northwest. We will be moving in a southeasterly direction. Within the site, apart from the buildings that belong to the Archaic, Hellenistic and Roman periods, we will be looking at the ruins of three churches.

The first of these lies to the left of the entrance. This was an early Christian basilica of the 4th/5th century, dedicated to the Archangel Michael. The Byzantine chapel of Ayios Stephanos was erected on the ruins of this basilica at a later date.

Our tour of the archaeological site begins with a visit to the Temenos of Artemidorus of Perge. Artemidorus, who came from Perge in Asia Minor, was the admiral of the fleet of the Ptolemies of Egypt. He founded the sanctuary at the end of the 4th or start of the 3rd century B.C.

The temenos is carved out of the rock. Its facade bears the chiselled figures of a dolphin, an eagle and a lion, the symbols of Poseidon, Zeus and Apollo respectively. The symbols of these gods, to the worship of whom the sanctuary was dedicated, are

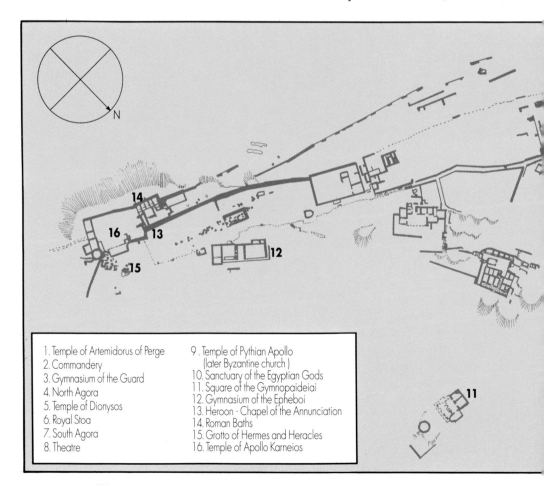

1. Temple of Artemidorus of Perge
2. Commandery
3. Gymnasium of the Guard
4. North Agora
5. Temple of Dionysos
6. Royal Stoa
7. South Agora
8. Theatre
9. Temple of Pythian Apollo (later Byzantine church)
10. Sanctuary of the Egyptian Gods
11. Square of the Gymnopaideiai
12. Gymnasium of the Epheboi
13. Heroon - Chapel of the Annunciation
14. Roman Baths
15. Grotto of Hermes and Heracles
16. Temple of Apollo Karneios

accompanied by inscriptions also chiselled into the rock. The sanctuary was also dedicated to the worship of other gods, namely Concord, Priapus, Hecate, the Kabeirians and the Dioskouroi. Exactly above the symbol of Poseidon is inscribed the figure of the sanctuary's founder, Artemidorus. Continuing our tour, we come to a building on our right which is called the Stratonas or Governor's Palace.

It stands on the highest point in the city, and the stepped road that starts at the main street leads right to its main entrance.

It consists of a series of rooms, which on three of the four sides border on a square courtyard.

A short distance south of the Stratonas is what has been named the Garrison of the Guard because of its layout.

This again has a large square courtyard, whose east side is closed by two rooms.

Following the main street, we come to a point where it becomes wider.

We have reached the Agora, the most important public space in Ancient Thera (and any ancient city). It lies practically in the centre of the town and is divided by the main street into a north and south section.

On the east side and on a lower level stretches one of the two residential neighbourhoods, while on the west there were temples and other public buildings. To the east there is an unrestricted view of the sea.

The agora is 111 metres long, its width varies from 17 to 30 metres.

Northwest of the North Agora, on our right, we come to three Roman

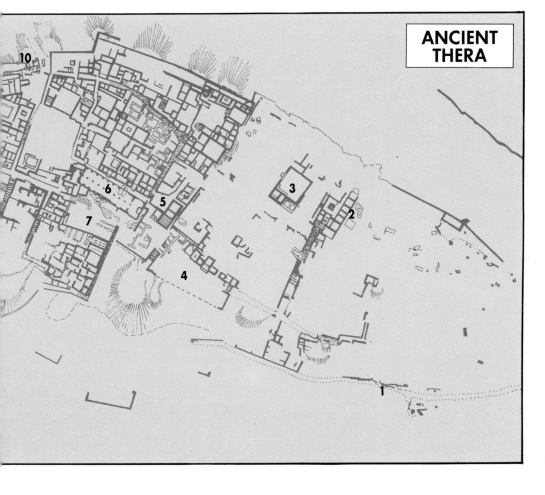

ANCIENT THERA

exedras or platforms and immediately afterwards the small Temple of Dionysos, where we climb up a broad stairway located on the side of the Agora. The temple dates from the Hellenistic period and consists of an antechamber (pronaos) and the temple proper (cella).

As we enter the South Agora, on our right we come to the so-called House of the Phallus, where there is a relief bearing the inscription "To my friends". Immediately beyond it is the Basilike or Royal Stoa, built in the 1st century A.D., during the reign of the Emperor Augustus. It is 46 metres long and 10 metres wide and has two entrances. The main entrance lies on the long side, the other on the narrow one. Its north section was specially arranged to house the statues of the imperial family. Its roof was supported by a central colonnade consisting of 10 Doric columns. At the point where the South Agora ends, the main street opens up again.

On our right we see the Sanctuary of the Egyptian Gods, Isis, Seraphis and Anubis, hollowed out of the rock.

To the southeast lies the Temple of Pythian Apollo, of which little remains because of the Byzantine church that was constructed on its foundations. On the left of the street stands the Theatre, preserved today with alterations carried out by the Romans, though it was erected in the 3rd century B.C. under the Ptolemies. Further south, behind the theatre, we come to the Roman Baths.

Further east is the chapel of the Evangelismos (Annunciation) of the Virgin. It was constructed upon a heroes' tomb of the 2nd century B.C., which is nevertheless still in good condition. Such tombs were usually

48

dedicated to the worship of the dead of the upper classes.

Continuing toward the southeast tip of the city, we come to the small Temple of Ptolemy III the Benefactor, then to the Column of Artemis, winding up at the most important spot in Ancient Thera, the Terrace of the Festivals. This was where the extremely old Doric rite of the Gymnopaideiai, dances by nude boys in honour of Apollo Karneios, took place.

Celebrated in Dorian settlements throughout Greece, it was the primary festival for the Therans, and graffiti on the walls indicate that it was going on as early as the 7th century B.C.

North of the Terrace of the Festivals stands the 6th century B.C. Sanctuary of Apollo Karneios. Its gate, which is on the terrace, leads to a rectangular courtyard with a cistern for collecting rainwater.

Southeast of the courtyard lies the priest's residence.

The temple, which opened to the northwest, is partly carved out of the rock, partly extends onto the terrace. It consists of a pronaos and cella, antechamber and temple proper.

South of the Terrace of the Festivals there is a small cave dedicated to the worship of Hermes and Heracles.

Finally, at the southeast tip of town, we come to the Gymnasium of the Epheboi, a 2nd century B.C. building, and adjacent to it a later addition to the Roman Baths.

▼ *Relief sculptures from the Temenos of Artemidoros. Carved into the rock are the lion of Apollo, the eagle of Zeus, the medallion of Artemidoros, who built the Temenos, and the dolphin of Poseidon.*

THE ARTS

The earliest art form found in Ancient Thera is pottery from the Geometric period. Thanks to the burial customs just described, many works of pottery have survived in reasonably good condition.

Theran ceramics of that period and later, which show an Anatolian style, were influenced by neighbouring Naxos. Nevertheless, the pottery from this time is perhaps the only work that can be attributed to Theran craftsmen.

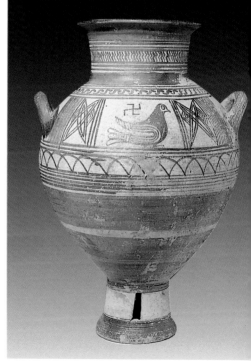

1. Statuette of a woman. The position of her hands indicates that she is in mourning (Athens, National Archaeological Museum).

2. Archaic jar with relief decoration (Archaeological Museum, Fira).

3,5,6. Theran vases of the Geometric and Archaic periods (Archaeological Museum, Fira).

4. Statuette of a lion (Archaeological Museum, Fira).

51

This is because from the 6th century B.C. and afterwards, the development of ceramics in other regions — Attica, Rhodes, Corinth, Ionia — and the location of Thera — on the crossroads of the trade routes — made it easy for the island to accept the wares of potters of other regions with the consequence that local production stagnated.

Some Middle Geometric vessels, a kind of drinking cup with two horizontal handles, have been preserved. Their linear decoration is placed directly on the clay. Examples of Late Geometric work exist in jugs and amphorae that were used as funerary urns. The amphorae were rather large in order to hold libations for the dead as well as the ashes. The amphora became the most characteristic pot made by Theran potters.

Apart from ceramics, examples of the plastic arts—sculptures — have also been found in Thera. Although it

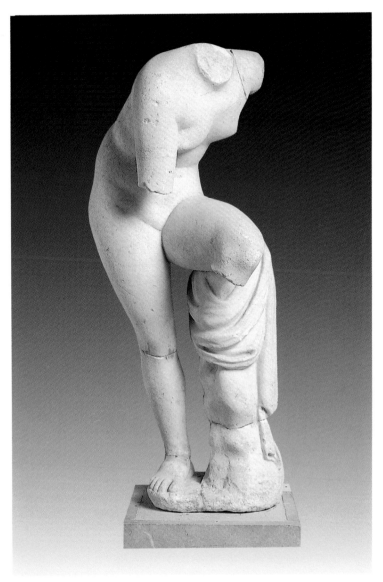

developed after pottery, perhaps
because of the absence of the raw
materials needed, such as marble,
Thera has given us some of the most
memorable works of ancient sculpture
that we know.

The two kouroi from the second half of
the 7th century B.C., now in the Fira
Archaeological Museum, and the kouros
in the National Archaeological Museum
in Athens, a work of the early 6th
century B.C. known as the Apollo of

Thera, are certainly among the best of
their kind. All three must have originally
stood over tombs in the ancient
cemetery at Sellada. The two first must
have been about 2 metres in height and
were made of thick grained island
marble.

◄ 1. The castle of Skaros.

► 2. The goulas or defence tower of Nimborio or Emborio.

Castles and Towers

During the Byzantine era and later during the Frankish occupation, the coasts of the Aegean suffered from incessant pirate raids.

To protect themselves from this threat, the islanders, especially, built or moved their settlements to inaccessible spots and fortified them for even greater security.

They also constructed watchtowers at high places, a kind of distant early warning system. In the Santorini of the 17th century, as we learn from the journals of the foreign travellers of the day, there were five such fortified settlements, the so-called castles.

The most important, thanks largely to its position, was at Skaros, which was called simply "The Castle" or "Kastro" in Greek.

Its 200 houses were perched on the summit of a steep, well defended rocky promontory.

To reach its walls a walk of at least half an hour was required.

A large bell, which was hung at the top of the rock, warned the inhabitants of impending danger.

Skaros was where the Latin lords, island officials and the Catholic archbishop resided; it was the medieval capital of Thera.

After 1700, when the pirate threat began to diminish, the Kastro gradually fell into ruin. Its inhabitants founded a new settlement, Fira, at a lower point.

The castle of Epanomeria or Apano Merias stood at the place occupied by present day Ia. It was also known as the castle of St. Nicholas.

The other three castles were situated in the south part of Santorini. Pyrgos (Tower) or Kainouryiopyrgos (New Tower) was erected during Byzantine times at the heart of the village of the same name.

The villagers would flee there in the event of enemy attack.

It was here that the representative of the Ottoman authorities would stay on his biannual visit to the island to administer justice.

It had about 100 houses and four churches, Ayios Iakovos, Ayios Ioannis the Theologian, Ayia Triada and the Theotaki, which was a small square church, with a dome and frescoes.

The castle of Nimborio or Emborio,

with 80 houses, was where commercial transactions took place. Finally, there was the castle of Akrotiri or Poundas, on the cape, with about 200 houses, of which only a few ruins remain today.

Apart from the fortified settlements or castles, Santorini also had a good many "goulades", isolated defence towers that stood either inside or outside of the fortress walls.

These were used as places for storage of foodstuffs or lodging for the feudal lords, as well as refuges in case of enemy attack.

We know that there were such towers at Epanomeria (Ia), of which only the base has survived, at Nimboreio, which was built at the outskirts of the settlement and has been preserved almost intact, at Akrotiri at the centre of the castle and, finally, at Fira.

The islanders who did not have access to sanctuary in the castles or goulades during enemy raids used to hide in the caves which abound on the island.
The watchtowers were manned by sentinels who kept a sharp watch over their districts and warned the people when pirates appeared on the horizon.

▲ *The goulas or defence tower of Epanomeria or Ia.*

*The lines
bow in humility
and culminate in domes.*

Vernacular and Ecclesiastical Architecture

The singular topography of Santorini has contributed decisively to the evolution of its special indigenous architecture. Its characteristic architectural style, although belonging generally to the architecture of the Aegean, has developed and at the same time projected many individual features and forms that show particular plasticity. And this because it has exploited the unusual landscape and possibilities of the place. The construction materials used by the local craftsman in building are exclusively volcanic in origin. They include black stone, red stone, pumice, lava, ash, and pozzuolana. Houses roofed with cylindrical or cross vaults and houses dug out of the vertical face of the lava cliffs are the principal building types on the island. The dugout structure illustrates the ingenuity of the locals in the search for easy, inexpensive housing. The vaulting is a consequence of the need for a substitute for wood, which

is nonexistent on the island. In their present form, the settlements on Thera can be separated into those built on the rim of the cliff facing the caldera, the so-called linear settlements of Fira, Ia and Therasia; those that developed outside the walls of the castles in various directions, the expanded fortress villages of Pyrgos, Emborio and Akrotiri; and the dug-out or troglodyte neighbourhoods. These are the settlements that in their original form followed the banks of a riverbed and eventually spilled over into a more fertile district, as at Finikia, Vothonas, Karterado. In terms of construction methods, Santorini's houses fall into three categories: troglodyte, semi-built and built. The troglodyte dwellings are those which have been completely hollowed out of the volcanic earth, the semi-built have some added sections that have been constructed, and the last are those which have been constructed in the usual manner on the surface of the

land. The troglodyte houses, which belonged to the poorest of the islanders, were relatively long with a narrow frontage. This facade was always supplemented with a built wall, which closed the living area. They had a cylindrical roof, it too hollowed out of the lava. The resulting long, narrow space was divided by a built wall into two sections, the living area in front, the bedroom, less well lit, in back. Apart from the door, the built facade usually had three other symmetrical openings: a window on either side of the door and a kind of skylight shaped like a half-moon above the door. These apertures were repeated in the interior partition wall, bringing both light and air to the back room. The kitchen, with a fireplace for cooking, consisted of a low, built corner with a vaulted ceiling that was connected with the living area. The lavatory was located outside the house with access from the courtyard. The courtyard also usually contained a cistern, which was an indispensable part of every house,

1,2,3,4. The houses of Santorini are uncluttered, functional, completely at one with their location; some of their details are unique.

5. The church domes are often blue like the Aegean Sea.

rain being the only source of water on Santorini, as on many of the other Cyclades. In the semi-built houses, one side, generally that of the entrance, is constructed, while the rest has been dug out. The roof over the built sections may be a dome, cross vault or a kind of covering made of stones and pozzuolana — volcanic rock which can form a type of cement when pulverized and mixed with water — that was poured into a mould until

it hardened. As for the free-standing houses, these fall into three categories: farm houses, vernacular town houses, and the mansions of the more affluent. The farm house was situated outside the limits of town or village. It has a large courtyard and several auxiliary buildings (stable, chicken coop, oven, and inevitably a cistern or tank for collecting rain water). It may be either hollowed out or built, depending on its location. It

The imagination of the folk craftsman created simple yet unique doors, balconies overlooking the sea, and stairways leading to the sky.

usually has only one story, but this also is a function of the surrounding topography. The oven, which is cylindrical in shape, is normally placed in the courtyard. An indispensable complement in the majority of Santorini's farm houses, particularly those in areas where vines are cultivated, is the wine press. The wine press with its characteristic arched double door and the barrels or

"voutsia" as the locals call them, had several compartments. It was often lit by a hole in the middle of the roof, which could be closed from above with stones. The vernacular town houses, which stand in the centre of

Santorini's settlements where construction is dense, have limited space to work with. This is why they are frequently irregular in shape, consisting of many storeys, with auxiliary areas found on a different level in each house. There are fewer spaces for animals than in the farm house. And they all have the required furnishings: chests for clothes, linen, and food; tables, chairs, wooden sofas, sideboards, furniture that can be found all over the Aegean islands and that became "de rigeur" with the growth of shipping. It is common knowledge that the poorer families slept on the floor; for a long time, European-style beds were a luxury reserved to the rich. The mansion house, like the vernacular house, is found in the middle of the towns and villages. In its initial form it must have resembled its humbler counterpart, as both house types evolved from the dwellings constructed within the castle precincts. Their imposing size and symmetrical facades, which are their most obvious features today, must have been acquired later on. The

1,2,3,4. The bell towers are often stately and majestic.

5. The church domes are frequently surmounted by a lamp which is in turn topped by a second, smaller dome on which stands the cross.

monumental mansion houses are mainly a product of the 19th century, as can be seen from the dates inscribed above their doors. Their owners generally belonged to the merchant class, as maritime trade was flourishing by that time. Their design must have been Italian in origin, based on Renaissance models. The facades of these houses are geometric, dressed with red chiselled stone. Their roofing consists of cross vaults and monastery-type domes, the so-called "skafes", which are covered by a terrace. The mansion house was so popular in Santorini, that the passion for the neoclassical style, so prevalent in other parts of Greece, never caught on there. There are some neighbourhoods in the settlements of Santorini that consist solely of mansion houses. Ia's Sidera district is where the 19th century sea captains built their homes. They placed them near the smooth, flat side of the town, where building is scattered; the dwellings of the crew members are located near the precipice, where the density is high and the houses dug out. At Messaria, too, the houses of the gentry stand in the central district. On Santorini, apart from the private ovens of the farm houses, there were buildings in the various neighbourhoods that functioned exclusively as ovens for the use of the community. These ovens, usually, were an annex of the baker's home, though in a few instances they were connected with a flourmill, and became known as the "mill house". More often, the mills were isolated structures situated outside residential areas. Nevertheless, in cases where the oven and mill functioned as a single unit, then the oven and the main dwelling would be built on a different

la. The houses follow the lie of the land, interacting with it to form a harmonious whole.

level from the mill, usually below the ground so as not to interfere with its operation. The mills of Santorini are the same as those found all over the Cyclades. They are cyclindrical with an articulated roof and the arms with the sails, which turn in all winds and move the top millstone. The rubbing of the top millstone on the bottom one grinds the wheat and other grains into flour. The churches of Santorini, although very much a part of the island's cubist architecture style, show a Western influence in their relatively large size. The volcano's eruptions and the catastrophic earthquakes that shattered the island from time to time strengthened the religious fervour of the locals, which intensified when they were confronted with Catholicism during the Frankish occupation. Thus, before the 1956 earthquake, the island boasted some 260 churches. Most of those that have survived are

of the one-aisled basilica type with dome, while others are cruciform in shape with dome. The dome, which may be white, as in most of the churches, or blue, is frequently ridged rather than smooth. Sometimes it is capped by a lantern, a clearly Renaissance touch. The facade of the churches and cathedrals alike is dominated by the presence of twin bell towers. Santorini's monasteries are massive, often reminiscent of fortresses, such as the monastery of Prophitis Elias. They have an inner courtyard, arcades and impressive bell towers.

*F*ira

Fira, also known as Hora, is the capital of Santorini. It has a permanent population of 1,718 residents (1990 census) and is built on the precipice, on the rim of the caldera some 260 metres above sea level.

The volcano lies exactly opposite, still emitting puffs of steam.

The town dates from 1810, when the inhabitants of Skaros — no longer terrified by the pirate threat — began to abandon the castle and establish themselves in this lower flatter area, with access to the sea.

Fira is a long, narrow collection of buildings with steep, narrow, stepped alleyways.

The houses on the caldera side are dug-out dwellings, constructed on different levels, one above the other, so that the roof of one forms the courtyard of the next.

You can reach the town by car or bus from Athinios, Fira's port and the

The settlement seems to spill over the rim of the caldera.

island's only harbour where ships can dock. It can also be reached from Mesa Yialos, the spot usually chosen by the cruiseships.

From here the ascent up the 500 or so steps to Fira may be made by funicular, walking or on donkeyback. The spectacular architecture of its dazzling white houses, that seem to cling to the dark sides of the caldera, and the incomparable view of the volcano and the open sea combine to make Fira one of the most breathtakingly beautiful places on earth.

Among its best preserved districts is Kato Fira.

The churches of Ayios Menas and Christos are located here, both masterpieces of ecclesiastical architecture, the former with its typical Santorinian dome, the latter with its exquisitely carved iconostasis and

Fira is one "picture" after another. For an unforgettable experience, take a donkey ride from Mesa Yialos down by the shore up to town.

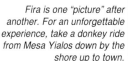

bishop's throne.

On the border between the Catholic and Orthodox quarters stands Fira's Archaeological Museum.

It houses the finds from the excavations at Akrotiri and Mesa Vouno, including: - vases and idols of the Early Cycladic period (2500-2000 B.C.) - pottery from Akrotiri (1500 B.C.) - Geometric and Attic vases and idols of the 8th and 7th century B.C. - sculpture of the Archaic, Hellenistic and Roman periods.

There are two Catholic convents in the Catholic quarter, belonging to the Sisters of Mercy, founded in 1841, and the Dominicans, where the Greek Handicrafts Organization has a school for carpet weaving.

Apart from the sights it has to offer, Fira is the centre of life on Santorini.

There are numerous hotels, restaurants, bars, cafes and discos to satisfy the visitor, as well as shops selling folk arts and crafts — pottery and hand-woven fabrics — and pricey gold jewelry.

Fira changes at dusk. Tha dazzling sun withdraws. The lights are lit and before long the quiet of the semi-darkness will surrender to the sounds from the tavernas, the cafes and the discos.

Firostefani

Nearby, and by now an extension of Fira, Firostefani is another long, narrow settlement built alongside the rim of the caldera. Boasting a superb view of the volcano, it has a picturesque square, a church dedicated to St. Gerasimos — the only one on the island surrounded by cypress trees — hotels and restaurants. Between Firostefani and Imerovigli or Merovigli, which is the next settlement on the caldera rim, stands the old Orthodox monastery of Ayios Nikolaos. It was founded by the Ghizi rulers and was originally located at Skaros.

Firostefani could be called the "balcony over the Aegean". Palia and Nea Kammeni lie directly opposite.

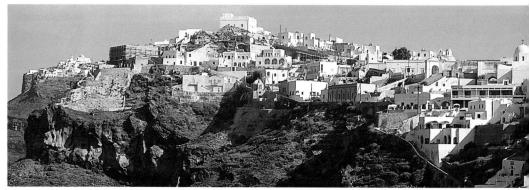

Imerovigli

The name of this village belongs to the days of the pirates:
"vigla" = watchtower, "imera" = day. Truly, its position at the centre and highest point along the caldera gave it visual command of the whole area, able to signal timely warnings to the population when pirates sailed into view. It also derived importance from its proximity to the fortress at Skaros. Imerovigli's church of Malteza has a marvelous carved iconostasis with icons depicting scenes from the Old Testament. There is a path from Imerovigli leading to Skaros.

Skaros

Up here you can see what remains of the old castle. The path, which heads south initially and then bears west, terminates at the white-washed chapel of the Virgin Theoskepasti, which looks as though it has been hollowed out of the rock.

1,2,3,4. Imerovigli means "day watch". Here too the same images are repeated: Simple houses and balconies overlooking the sea.

5. Skaros was the islanders' most important fortress. Very little remains to indicate its past glory.

*I*a

Sometimes referred to as Apano Meria, Ia is linked with 10 kilometres of paved road to Fira and faces Therasia. As mentioned above, Apano Meria is a collection of six villages: Ia, Perivola, Finikia, Tholos on the ridge and Ammoudi and Armeni at the base of the caldera. Ia is built at a lower altitude than Fira, nearer the sea, to which it is connected by two sets of cobbled steps. The one to Ammoudi has 214 steps, the other to Armeni has 286. Down at Armeni, looking as though it has been hollowed out of the rock, stands the little church of Ai Nikolas, protector of seafarers, a short distance from the coast.

The existence of Ia is referred to well before 1650. Under the Franks, it was the capital of one of the five administrative districts into which Santorini was divided. Ia knew its

Ia also spills over the rim of the caldera to gaze at Fira opposite.

greatest prosperity in the late 19th-early 20th century. Its economic development was based on its merchant fleet, which plied the Eastern Mediterranean from Alexandria to the Crimea. In 1890, it boasted 2,500 inhabitants and 130 of the ships in Santorini's fleet belonged to people from Ia, while there was a small shipyard at Armeni. Today Ia is Santorini's second largest village. It is less cosmopolitan than Fira, but in its way it is more picturesque and is without doubt one of the most

Every nook and cranny of Ia is a poem: the donkey's hooves clicking on the cobblestones, the moon shining dimly in the sky, the windmills descending the hillside, the little table for breakfast and afternoon coffee.

beautiful places on the island. It has a great many troglodyte houses, carved out of the cliffside by the crews of the merchant ships for their families.

The two-storey captains' houses, built at the highest part of the village, are a reflection of its former affluence.

Finally, there are its churches and its splendid sunsets, which bathe the hills and buildings in a purple glow when the sun sinks into the Aegean.

Ia's roads are laid with marble plaques rather than the cobblestones encountered elsewhere on the island.

Of the castle that once defended Ia, only a few stones remain; the same is true of the tower that stood on the highest spot in the vicinity.

Inside the tumbled walls of the castle, on the edge of the cliff, there is a church dedicated to the Virgin of Platsani.

Ia has a small museum of maritime history.

Churches with blue and white domes pop up from among the houses.

Messaria

Messaria lies 3.5 kilometres south of Fira, in the interior of the island, amidst vineyards and vegetable gardens.
Much of Santorini's wonderful wine is produced here.
With a permanent population of about 400, Messaria also has a number of hotels and restaurants to house and feed summer visitors.

Vothonas

Picturesque Vothonas, built up the hillside like an amphitheatre to the east of Messaria, is almost an extension of its neighbour. In this farming village, which has 300 inhabitants, you'll find a church dedicated to St. Anne, with a lovely carved iconostasis bedecked with icons depicting scenes from the Old Testament.

Exo Gonia

South of Vothonas is Exo Gonia, a small village that seems to climb up the mountainside. Worth a visit here is its church of Ayios Charalambos.
Built on a height, it can seen from virtually every corner of the island.

1. Messaria.
2. Vothonas.

*P*yrgos

Built at the foot of Prophitis Elias, Pyrgos is an example of a settlement that was fortified in the Middle Ages; it is the only village in Santorini where the medieval features and atmosphere have been so vividly preserved. Its streets, which follow the contours of the hillside, divided the village into zones. The walls of the outermost houses were an integral part of the village fortifications. When the danger of pirate raids diminished, the inhabitants started to build homes outside the walls, giving the village its present form. There are many churches worth seeing in Pyrgos. The oldest, known as the Theotaki, is dedicated to the Dormition of the Virgin. It was erected in the 11th century a little after the church of Episkopi at Mesa Gonia. Between 1537 and 1650, other churches were built: the Metamorphosis (Transfiguration) of the Saviour, Ayia Theodosia and the "dug-out" church of Ayios Nikolaos of Kissira. The church

of the Eisodia tis Theotokou (Presentation of the Virgin) with its carved iconostasis joined them between 1650 and 1664. Later additions were Ayia Aikaterini (1660), Ayios Georgios (1680), Archangel (Taxiarchis) Michael (1690), Ayios Nikolaos (1700), and numerous others. Near Pyrgos, crowning Mt. Prophitis Elias, is a monastery dedicated to the prophet. The solid facade of its exterior walls perforated with just a few windows is reminiscent of a fortress. It was founded in 1711 and built in two phases, 1711 to May 1724 and November 1852 to March 1857. The carved iconostasis in the monastery church is a fine example of the genre. The monastery was subject to the Patriarchate of Constantinople. Until 1860 it was cenobitic, while until 1853 no women were permitted to enter it. In earlier times, the monastery of Prophitis Elias possessed considerable wealth. It even had its own ship which

View of Pyrgos, with
Fira in the background.

conducted trade for the benefit of the monastery. At the same time, it was also an active intellectual and patriotic influence. From 1806 to 1845 it ran a school where Greek language and literature were taught to children. The monastery's decline began in 1860. Its buildings suffered serious damage in the earthquakes of 1956. Today the monastery has an important collection of ecclesiastical objects, manuscripts and old and more recent books, as well as ethnographic material. Near Mesa Gonia, a farming village with a wine production and storage plant, is the most important Byzantine monument on the island, the church of the Panayia Piskopi or Episkopi Gonia. Founded by the emperor Alexis I Komninos in the 11th century, it is dedicated to the Dormition of the Virgin. At some point in its history it

may have been used as a Catholic
monastery and it also served as the
seat of the bishop of Santorini. It has
undergone many alterations and
additions, however, since the 11th
century. The only thing that has
remained intact from that time is its
carved marble iconostasis. The
frescoes have been dated to ca. 1100.

*Pyrgos was a fortified village,
the only one on the island
to have retained its strong
mediaeval features.*

Athinios

This picturesque cove, located about 11 kilometers from Fira, constitutes the island's only harbour. A few houses have sprung up around it, along with a few tavernas. To the right of the quay is a pretty, small, pebbly beach.

Megalohori

Situated to the south of Athinios, this inland village belies its name ("Big Village"), having only some 250 inhabitants.

1. One example of ecclesiastical architecture in Santorini is the belltower at Megalohori.

3, 4. Athinios.

5. The beautiful red beach.

1	4
2	5
3	

Emborio

The largest village in the south part of the island stands in the heart of a fertile plain.

During the Venetian occupation, Emborio was one of Santorini's five castles as well as being its trading centre, as its name implies (Emborio = trade, commerce in Greek). On the mountain opposite, you can still see the windmills that also contributed to the prosperity of the district.

Strangely, the population of Emborio, the so-called "Boryiani", were also seafarers. The village port was at Perissa. In former times a man with a lantern used to walk from house to house before dawn to wake up the fishermen — a kind of community alarm clock.

A bit before the entrance to the village there is a little church dedicated to St. Nicholas Marmaritis. It is virtually attached to the ruins of an ancient temple to Thea Basilica (the mother of the gods), built in the 3rd century B.C. The church takes its name from the grey chiselled marble of which the temple was made.

Perissa

One of the most popular beaches on Santorini and one of the most geared to tourism, Perissa has coarse black sand. The east side of the beach is overshadowed by the dark hulk of Mesa Vouno. Perissa is well endowed with hotels, fast food establishments and restaurants, designed to make your stay even more pleasant. There are also two churches worth seeing, the Holy Cross (Timios Stavros) and Ayia Irini (late 16th-early 17th century).

Kamari

This was the port for Ancient Thera and in those days it was called Ia. Today it is the second most popular beach on the island. The extended beach with its fine black sand is protected to the south by the vertical mass of Mesa Vouno. Here, apart from clear water for swimming, you'll find all kinds of hotels, tavernas, restaurants, discos, a campsite, bars and a cinema.

The Volcano

Its crater lies at Nea Kammeni, the islet formed by the most recent eruptions of the volcano.

It is a mass of black substance, which is simply lava that poured as a viscous liquid from the bowels of the earth and then hardened.

The caique that will take you there anchors off the coast of the little island, where the water is warm and a translucent green due to the sulphur content.

From the beach there is a path right up to the rim of the crater.

The walk takes about half an hour. Near the crater, puffs of steam smelling strongly of sulphur are emitted from cracks at many points. For your walk to the crater, don't forget to wear rubber-soled shoes and take a good supply of drinking water.

A visit to Nea Kammeni to see the volcano's crater is a unique experience.

116

*T*herasia

The area of this island is no more than 16 square kilometres (5.7 km. long, 2.7 km. at its broadests).
This remnant of the west coast of prehistoric Strongyle is home today to some 250 people.
Although it has the same geographical configuration as Santorini, it has not experienced the same rapid tourist development.
The west coast of the island slopes gently into the sea, backed by a fertile valley where the inhabitants, farmers for the most part, grow grapes, split yellow peas, barley and tomatoes.
The east coast, in contrast, ends abruptly in steep cliffs.
The island's biggest village, also called Therasia, is built at the rim of the precipice. Two hundred and seventy steps link it to the coast and the tiny harbour. Here, you'll encounter the same cobbled paths, the same architecture and the same, spectacular view of the caldera as on the larger island.
There are two other hamlets on Therasia, Potamos with 90 inhabitants and Agrilia, which is deserted.
On the south coast of the island, near the sea, there is a cave called Trypiti (which means "perforated"), while to the north stands the chapel dedicated to St. Irene, which gave Santorini its name.

Useful Information

HOW TO GET THERE

By ferryboat:
Ferries leave Piraeus daily bound for Santorini (distance 130 nautical miles). The trip lasts about 12 hours. You can get to Piraeus from central Athens by metro (with stops at Victoria, Omonia, Monastiraki, etc.) or bus. For information about ferry schedules from Piraeus to Santorini, call the Piraeus port authority (01)451.1311.

By plane:
Santorini is linked with Athens by daily Olympic Airlines flights. For information, call Olympic Airlines, Athens (01)966.6666. The flight lasts about one hour. There are also direct flights between Mykonos, Heraklion, Rhodes and Santorini, while many charter flights connect the island with major European cities. Santorini's airport is about 7 kilometres from Fira. Olympic Airlines buses carry passengers to and from the airport free of charge.

INTER-ISLAND CONNECTIONS:

Ferries connect Santorini regularly with the following islands: Ios, Naxos, Paros, Syros, Sikinos, Folegandros, Sifnos, Serifos, Kimolos, Milos, Mykonos, and Heraklion, Crete. For information. call the harbour master at Santorini (0286)22.239. You can also fly to Mykonos, Heraklion and Rhodes. For information, call the OA offices in Athens (01)966.6666 or at Santorini (0286)22.493.

STAYING ON THE ISLAND
Accommodation:
Accommodation is available in a wide range of hotels, pensions, guest houses, bungalows, and furnished apartments, which are divided into five categories and are found in the large villages on Santorini. There are also two campsites, one at Kamari (capacity 570 people, 0286/31.451) and the other at Perissa (capacity 249 people, 0286/81.343). You can also rent a whole villa or a room in a private home. For a stay in exceptionally pleasant, traditional surroundings, the GNTO has restored some old houses in Ia and converted them into pensions. Not only do they

have a stupendous view of the caldera, they are also fully equipped for self-catering. For information, call (0286)71.016, 71.234. For more information regarding hotel accommodation, get in touch with the Hotel Chamber of Greece, 24 Stadiou St., tel: (01)323.6962, telex: 214.269 XEPE GR, fax: (01)322.5449, P.O. Box XENEPEL.

For on the spot reservations, the GNTO has a branch office at Karageorgi Servias and 2 Stadiou streets on Constitution Square (inside the National Bank of Greece), tel: (01)323.7193 from Monday to Friday, 08.00 - 14.00.

The Tourist Police on Santorini will also help you find a place to stay.

GETTING AROUND ON THE ISLAND

There are buses between Fira and Imerovigli-Vourvoulo-Ia/ Messaria-Pyrgos-Akrotiri/ Messaria-Pyrgos-Megalohori-Emborio- Perissa/ Kamari/ Monolithos. There are also a number of taxis (0286/22.555) and several rent-a-car or rent-a-motorbike agencies. Organized excursions to the most important sites are offered by the island's travel agencies, which are listed below:

At Fira:
Aloni Tours (81.665),
Arkadia Lines (23.210),
Atlantis (22.965), Belonias (22.221),
Contact Travel (23.562),
CycladesTravel (23.512), Dakoutzos (22.958), Damigos (22.473),
Mendrinos
Travel (22.989),
Meridian Travel (22.635),
More of Santorini (22.007),
Pelekan (22.940), Santorama (23.177), Santo Volcano (22.177),
Skaros Travel (22.643)
Spectrum (23.088), X-ray (22.624).

At Kamari:
Hephaistos Travel (31.708),
Thera Tours (31.131),
Kamari (31.445),
Matina Travel (31.860),
Nomikos Travel (23.660).

At Ia:
Karvounis Tours (71.209),
Santorini (71.214).

At Perissa:
Romani Tours (81.177),
Santosan Travel (81.456).
From Skala below Fira caiques depart for Therasia, Palia and Nea Kammeni. You can also get a caique for Therasia from Ia.

Where to go for entertainment

There are restaurants serving European style cuisine as well as Greek tavernas in all the villages on the island. In the more frequented places, such as Ia, Perissa, Kamari and Emborio, you'll find discos and bars to complement your nightlife, while at Emborio and Pyrgos there are nightclubs with live "bouzoukia" shows. Fira has an almost unlimited choice of restaurants and entertainment spots. Eating out can range from the most sophisticated French restaurant, to a traditional taverna, a pizzeria, souvlaki stand or a fast food joint. You'll spend many pleasant evenings sampling the bars and pubs, discos and live music clubs or viewing a film in an open-air cinema. But even if you're only on Santorini for a short while, don't fail to enjoy an ouzo or a cup of coffee in one of the cafes overlooking the sea and the volcano. Island delicacies worth tasting include fava (pureed split yellow peas served with a little oil, lemon and chopped onion), domatokeftedes (rissoles made of tomatoes, flour, onions, and herbs), chloro (a fresh, particularly delicious local cheese), and the famous Santorini wine.

Throughout the year there are "paniyiria" — saints' days celebrated with abundant food and drink and folk music played on traditional instruments to accompany dancing. Among the most important of these are:

- Prophitis Elias, July 20, at Fira.
- The feast of the Virgin, August 15 and the Transfiguration of the Saviour, August 6, at Akrotiri.
- The Virgin of Episkopi, August 15 and the Virgin Myrtidiotissa, September 24, at Kamari.
- The Purification of the Virgin, February 2, at Ia.
- St. John's day, August 29, at Perissa, where local fava, olives, wine and bread are offered to all present.

SPORTS

The main sport that one enjoys on Santorini is of course swimming. Windsurfing equipment can be rented at Kamari. Santorini is also a wonderful place for hiking. There are so many things to explore on this fascinating island, and walking is the best way to really get to know a place.

SHOPPING

Local products worth buying on the island include the various kinds of Santorini wine — brusco, "bordeaux", vinsanto, nychteri — tomato paste and sun-dried tomatoes, and split yellow peas (fava). There are also handicrafts, such as handwoven rugs (on order from the Rug-making School at Fira) and embroideries, etc. Other good buys are gold jewelry and paintings by Greek and foreign artists, many of whom have taken their inspiration from Santorini's striking scenery and architecture.

WHAT ELSE YOU SHOULD KNOW

Fira and Ia both have OTE (Greek Telephone Organization) centres, where you can make local and long distance telephone calls and send telegrams anywhere in the world.
OTE Fira, 22.399
OTE IA, 71.242
Open from October - June 15 from 07.30-22.00 from June 16 - September 30 from 07.30-24.00 Closed on weekends. At Fira, Ia and Pyrgos there is a post office. There is a Health Centre at Fira (22.237), while rural clinics may be found at Emborio (81.126), Ia (71.227), Pyrgos (31.207) and Therasia (23.191). Fira has several pharmacies. There are petrol stations and autorepair shops at Fira, Kamari and Pyrgos. Akrotiri and Karterado also have autorepair shops. In Greece, apart from the "movable" holidays of Clean Monday (the beginning of Lent), Good Friday, Easter, and Easter Monday and Whitmonday, the following official holidays are celebrated:

Jan.	Mar.	May	Aug.	Oct.	Dec.
1,6	25	1	15	28	25,26

Banking hours are Monday-Thursday: 08.14.00; Friday: 08.00-13.30.
All petrol stations are open Monday-Friday from 07.00-19.00; Saturday from 07.00-15.00, while some are open in the evenings (until midnight) and on Sundays (07.00-19.00) on a rotating basis. All pharmacies are open from Monday to Friday (normal shop hours), while there is always one on duty on nights and weekends on a rotating basis.

USEFUL TELEPHONE NUMBERS

Area code for Santorini (0286)
Police Department 22.649
Town Hall, Fira 22.231

Town Hall, Ia 71.228
GNTO office 71.234, 71.016
Olympic Airlines (agent) 22.493,
22.793, 22.218
Olympic Airlines (airport) 31.525
Harbour Master 22.239
Archaeological Museum, Fira 22.217
Archaeological Site, Akrotiri 81.366
Maritime Museum, Ia 71.156

Therasia:

OTE centre 23.022, 23.190
Rural clinic 23.191
Anyone with a yacht should anchor it
at Fira (Athinios).
For information, call the harbour
master (listed above).

HOTELS

K	N/L	TEL.	BEDS.
Fira or Chora (0286)			
A	Atlantis		42
A	Villa Theoxenia (P)	22.950	12
B	Villa Renos (P)	22.369	13
B	Porto Fira (F.A.)	22.849	14
C	Antonia	22.879	20
C	Dedalos	22.834	40
C	Hellas	22.782	27
C	Erolia	22.155	32
C	Theoxenia	22.740	20
C	Kavalari	22.455	39
C	Kallisti Thira	22.317	64
C	Panorama	22.481	34
C	Pelikan	23.113	34
C	Porto Karras	22.979	16
D	Anatoli	22.307	21
D	Leto	22.540	22
D	Loukas	22.480	35
D	M.P. Apartments (F.A.)	22.752	12
D	Santorini	22.593	46
D	Tataki	22.389	18
D	Flora	81.524	14
E	Asimina	22.034	26
E	Vina	-	22
E	Thirasia	22.546	33
E	Keti	22.324	17
E	Katris	22.842	15
E	Lignos	23.101	15
Akrotiri (0286)			
C	Akrotiri	81.375	30
C	Goulielmos	81.615	54
D	Paradisos	81.352	28
Vothonas (0286)			
B	Mediterranean Beach	31.167	80
C	Markisia	31.583	31
Vourvoulos (0286)			
B	Santorini Villas (F.A.)	22.036	14
Emborio			
D	Archaia Elefsina	81.250	28

HOTELS

K	N/L	TEL.	BEDS.
Exo Gonia (0286)			
A	Nano (F.A.)	31.001	18
C	Makarios	31.375	54
Imerovigli (0286)			
A	Altana Apartments (T. F.A.)	23.240	30
A	Iliotopos (F.A.)	23.670	17
B	Angeliki (F.A.)	-	7
B	Arts Apartments (F.A.)	23.528	10
B	Kelly's (F.A.)	-	6
B	Skaros Villas (F.A.)	23.153	13
C	Thanos Villas (F.A.)	22.883	31
C	Honeymoon Villas (F.A.)	23.058	20
E	Katerina	22.708	18
Kamari (0286)			
A	Kallisti Villas (G.A)	-	20
A	Belonia Villas (F.A.)	31.138	26
B	Delfinia (F.A.)	31.302	36
B	Iliachtida	31.394	68
B	Rivari Santorini (H & B)	31.687	42
B	Rousos Beach	31.255	72
B	Christos (G.A)	-	40
C	Akis	31.670	24
C	Alkyon	31.295	28
C	Argyros (F.A.)	-	30
C	Argo	31.374	33
C	Artemis Beach	31.198	54
C	Astro	31.336	68
C	Avra	31.910	35
C	Vatos	31.660	54
C	Zefyros	31.108	44
C	Kamari Beach	31.243	93
C	Kapetan Yiannis (F.A.)	31.154	30
C	Kastelli	31.122	20
C	Matina	31.491	52
C	Orion	31.182	41
C	Poseidon	31.698	60
C	Tropical Beach	31.789	43
D	Akropol	31.012	30
D	Andreas	31.692	63
D	Aspro Spiti	31.441	29
D	Golden Sun	31.301	30
D	Blue Sea	31.481	49

K	N/L	TEL.	BEDS.
D	Nikolina I	31.253	64
D	Sigalas	31.260	23
D	Ta Kymata	31.694	42
D	Tareli	31.773	43
E	Villa Elli	31.266	23
E	Yannis Kapelos	31.166	16
E	Dionysios	31.310	16
E	Nikolina	31.253	17
E	Nina	31.697	24
E	Prekamaria	31.266	22

Karterados (0286)

K	N/L	TEL.	BEDS.
B	Santorini Tennis Club (F.A.)	22.122	22
C	Albatros	23.435	73
C	Londos	22.146	39
D	Cyclades	22.948	32
D	Babis	22.314	41
D	Olympia	22.213	56
D	Palladion	22.583	22
E	Karterados	22.489	17
E	Nikos	23.737	43
E	O Yannis	22.552	12
E	Tzina	22.834	20

Kondohori

K	N/L	TEL.	BEDS.
D	Anatoli	22.307	21
E	Vina	22.483	22

Megalohori (0286)

K	N/L	TEL.	BEDS.
A	Villa Dolphin (T. P.)	81.663	12
C	Santorini Star	81.198	25

Messaria (0286)

K	N/L	TEL.	BEDS.
A	Santorini Image	31.874	228
C	Anny	31.626	77
C	Artemidoros	31.640	30
C	Loizos	31.733	23
D	Apollon	31.792	24
E	Andreas	31.693	28

Ia (0286)

K	N/L	TEL.	BEDS.
A	Kanaves Ia (F.A.)	71.453	17
A	Perivolas (T. F.A.)	71.308	14
A	Stoa (F.A.)	-	10
B	Atlantis Villas (F.A.)	71.214	38
B	Golden Sunset Villas (P.)		-

K	N/L	TEL.	BEDS.
B	Irene (F.A.)	-	13
B	Katikies (F.A.)	71.401	14
B	Laokasti Villas (F.A.)	-	10
B	Laounda (P)	71.204	20
C	Ethrio Santorinis (F.A.)	71.217	19
C	Ia's Sunset (F.A.)	71.420	36
C	Finikia	71.373	27
D	Anemomylos	71.420	17
D	Fregata	71.221	40
E	Anemones	71.220	19
	GNTO Traditional Settlement	71.234	31

Perissa (0286)

K	N/L	TEL.	BEDS.
C	Eleni	81.627	25
C	Thira Mare	81.114	59
D	Zortzis	81.104	19
D	Marianna	81.286	20
D	Santa Irini	81.226	31
D	Christina	81.362	16
E	Marousianna	81.124	12
E	Boubis	81.203	29
E	Meltemi	81.325	38
E	Nota	81.209	12
E	Perissa	-	84
E	Rena	81.316	27
E	Chrysi Ammos	81.109	35

Pyrgos (0286)

K	N/L	TEL.	BEDS.
C	Zorbas	31.433	59

Firostefani (0286)

K	N/L	TEL.	BEDS.
A	Tsitouras (F.A.)	23.747	10
C	Galini	22.095	13
C	Galini II	22.095	13
C	Dana Villas (T. F.A.)	22.566	17
C	Ira (F.A.)	23.488	13
C	Kafieris	22.189	20
C	Nikolaos Kafieris	22.059	13
D	Efterpis Villas	22.541	13
E	Afrodite	22.161	20
E	Iliovasilema	23.046	15
E	Thira	22.863	20
E	Margarita	22.764	34
E	Mylos	22.173	13
E	Σοφία	22.802	12